WE ARE THE CHAMPIONS NOW

TD Ameritrade park
OMAHA

WE ARE THE CHAMPIONS NOW

And other poems

BY SEDGIE TAYLOR

Kimberly Carlisle Coghlan, Editor

Copyright @ 2021 by Sedgie Taylor

All rights reserved. No part of this book may be reproduced in any manner whatsoever without written permission except in the case of brief quotations embodied in critical articles and reviews.

First Printing, 2021

For my mother, Inez McAdams Taylor

We are the Champions Now

The stage is set for baseball
On this 30th day of June
The crack of bats, the flight of balls
The roars coming from the stadium soon.

Which player will shoulder his teammates?
Who will get the hero's call?
He anticipates the batter's box
As the umpire growls, "Play ball!"

Rowdey starts it with a hit to right
Come on, guys. Let's have some fun!
Rocker's error advances Jordan to third
Hancock's sac fly plates—run number one!

Will B continues his magic
Strikes out Vandy's fastest man.
Couple of walks raise the pressure.
The double play ruins Vandy's plans.

Rocker gets his taste of walks
A slow roller advances two.
Grounder to short produces another out
But plates the Bulldawgs' run #2.

Tall Man walks out of the box
Forsythe catches, after fighting the sun
Tall Man steals, number nine strikes out
And so does the very next one.

Center fielder proves that he is fast
Another fly ball hit and caught his way.
Three popups in this frame,
Easy inning for the first time today.

A packed house watches the out at first
Followed by Speedy getting out again.
Will B races to first for an out
Inning three is dust in the wind.

A leadoff single looks promising,
But Rocker grabs another gear
Striking out three in a row
Upcoming batters better watch it here

Number forty-three continues to show he's money
His defense has no flaw
Will B lobs an out to first
Hancock fields an out, tongue in jaw

Rowdey is safe, Allen's first hit!
Guys continue to light the torch
LoTan drives another grounder through
Bye-Bye, Rocker! Go sit on the porch.

Skinner catches one on the warning track
Another finds the middle of his glove
Chants of Maroon... White... echo loud
Strike Three! Love... love... love!

Lane gets out; Rowdey does too.
A grounder by first base, Allen gets two
Then Blondie confuses KJ6
And he ends up striking out too.

Skinner continues to make good catches
Kamren throws a dart!
Jordan covers centerfield for the last out
Seems Vandy has lost some heart.

LoTan goes deep, Scotty to first.
Skinner time... we'll take the call.
Blondie grooved the very next pitch
And Clark drives it over the wall

Sims takes the mound, churning a storm.
First batter—he strikes him out.
A ground out, another swing through the air
The dawgs are better, there's no doubt.

Ain't looking good for the Commodores
As they lazily cover the field
They make their routine plays, all right
But you can tell they're rocked and reeled

Sims keeps Vandy in the park
Ole' Skinner is having a good time.
I need to call an old friend of mine.
"Can somebody loan me a dime?"

Okay, Vandy has a shortstop
Our first two batters, he retires.
Lane gets a hit; Rowdey lines out
This team's still playing with fire.

Good defense beats good offense.
A great offense, tonight, will win.
These bulldawgs played together
Again... and again... and again!

These guys showed the world tonight
Good Golly, Miss Molly, just WOW!
Vandy, you can step down from the podium.
WE ARE THE CHAMPIONS NOW!

NCAA.com
#CWS
COLLEGE WORLD SERIES
THE GRE

Note from the Author

I was introduced to Mississippi State baseball back in my senior year of high school, in 1971. Having been raised twenty-three miles west of Starkville in the red, sandy hills of Choctaw County, we considered it a trip when we got to travel so far from home.

A friend of mine and I were riding in the bed of our buddy, George Ward's, truck, acting as bartenders for those in the cab.

Upon driving upon MSU property, off Highway 82, George steered onto a dirt road, headed south. He turned the truck right, into what looked like a cattle gap, continuing west until topping a hillside.

There, just ahead of us, we saw several trucks, with tailgates down, some spectators sitting on top of their cabs... and there was BASEBALL!

The clouds of dust rising from the playing field would settle upon the various vehicles and the needles of the cedar trees outside centerfield. As the game played on, frosty beverages consumed from the ice cooler helped wash down the dust that had accumulated in our throats.

I don't remember who played that day. I don't remember who won. But, from that point forward, I was hooked. MSU baseball had positioned a place in my heart.

Now, decades have passed, and players have come and gone. Crowds have increased. The stadium has grown. SEC championships have been won. Trips to Omaha have been made.

But no national title anointed... until now!! 2021! CWS National Champions!

George would be proud.

For Mother

Samuel Johnson once said, "Unless a man has courage, he has no security for preserving any other virtue."

My mother may have been the most courageous person I ever knew. From 1960-1971, she raised four children, alone. We learned the importance of family love, family values, and God's grace.

Her living example of how to treat people was a pattern of encouragement. She instilled in us children 4 questions to ask ourselves if we came upon a stumbling block in our progression of living.

What use is wisdom if I don't have the courage to act wisely?
What value is love if I don't have the courage to love?
What importance is truth if I don't have the courage to speak it?
Of what consequence is faith, without the courage to embrace it?

Therefore, courage activates all other goodness.

My mother encouraged me to write. It didn't matter about the subject. She always told me to never pass up a chance to write. She would say, "God gives different people different talents. He gave you a gift to write—use it!"

I wrote her several poems on Mother's Day throughout the years. She always looked forward to reading her cards before Sunday School class. I remember seeing tears streaming down her cheeks, and I'll never forget those appreciative hugs.

Now, she is no longer with us physically, but we feel her presence often. She was watching in spirit the night MSU won the national title—the night I was challenged to write the poem, from the opening pitch to the final out.

Mother loved MSU sports.

Her number one priority was to worship God. Second came loving her family. Her third priority was to treat her fellow man fairly, with respect. And last, but certainly not least, came the MSU Bulldogs.

Thank you, Mother.

I love you.

A Poem for Mom

As a youth, 'twas easy to follow
The paths her feet did trod
That led to life's adventures
That led to teachings of God

As a teen, self reliance took over
And she mustered a different approach.
She viewed my life from the sidelines:
Trained me daily, my teacher, my instructor... my coach

As an adult, we offered different opinions
Agreeing to sometimes disagree
And we did, but held no resentment
Not just mother and son... we were friends, you see.

The first Mother's Day I spent alone,
Selfishly, I was sad to see you go
The good days, I have solace in where you are.
And sad days are becoming rare as desert snow.

Poems for my Son

A young boy opened the front door
To a salesman, who tipped his hat
And asked the boy if he had a name
He answered, "Johnny Don't Do That!"

A lot of negative words
Find places to stick
In our hearts and our minds.
It's enough to make us sick.

We need positive words to influence life,
Words like love, can, and do.
When these words are repeated,
It will make life better for you.

The New Testament is testimony to freedom and hope,
Testimonies that can lift, not restrain.
The gospel is good news of promise
We learn from it again and again.

You haven't reached your harvest time.
It's still time for you to plant.
You should thank God daily
That you can do more than you can't.

~Written April 14, 1997

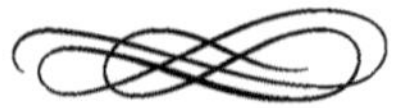

The Easter Bunny's comin,'
With lots of eggs to hide
I hope you find the ones
That are full of love inside.
Be good to those around you.
And say your prayers at night.
Just know that Jesus loves you,
And everything will be all right.

~Written for my 2-year-old son in 1995

Acknowledgments

To my Family,

My mother, Inez Taylor, for her encouragement

My brother, John Robert Taylor, gone but never forgotten

My sister, Barbara Porter Taylor, who was married to a bulldog fan

My sister, Kat wood, who shares my enthusiasm for baseball

My son, Joh Joseph Taylor—we couldn't help but love MSU sports. Could we?

My nephew, Chance Taylor, who texts me during the games

Continued...

To my friends,

Joey Long, who shared the love

Tyler Long, who introduced me the "The Loft"

Professor Gilbert, "Knock him out John"

The Abernathys, who shared their enthusiasm

The Judge, who donated his seats when not attending

Aaron W, whom I met at the Virginia Regional

Jerry S, who rode to Omaha with me in 2013

Jerry S' cousin Nancy, who contributed pictures

Stan Raye, for your support and contributing pictures

Candace, my bulldog buddy

Susie H, who sold me Notre Dame Regional Tickets

Barry C, saw him at every ballgame

And of course, the Candyman, a Mississippi State legend

www.ingramcontent.com/pod-product-compliance
Lightning Source LLC
Chambersburg PA
CBHW071459041025
33551CB00063B/1585